MORLEY HALL RULES

BY NUMBER 5

ISBN: 9798840799246
ISBN: 9798840799093

For all the Morley Hall Boys

CONTENTS

FOREWORD

Age twelve, in 1984, I was sent to Morley Hall Boarding School in Norfolk.

Morley Hall was not a private school, Borstal, youth detention centre or foster care. It was a special school owned and run by the Norfolk County Council Education Department—an institution like no other. As a last resort, when nothing else worked, and the system had no idea what was wrong, they packed you up and sent you off to Morley Hall.

Today the school is closed, and all its records have been destroyed. For the first time, I am going to write down the unwritten rules that controlled my life during my five-year stay at Morley Hall.

MORLEY HALL

Morley Hall is just south of Norwich between the towns of Wymondham and Attleborough. Set in acres of woodland, the three-story country house was built in 1841 in a late Georgian style; if you imagine an old English country hotel in the middle of nowhere, you have the right place.

The house has a long drive on both sides, just wide enough for one car and takes you through the woodland up to the grand house. Its main entrance has large white doors to welcome you.

The building itself is split into three floors, the ground floor with two large reception rooms, a dining room, a kitchen, and a hallway.

A grand oak staircase takes you up to the second floor with bedrooms and a large communal shower room and bathroom.

At the very top are the old servants' quarters

with more bedrooms and a communal shower and bathroom. From the back of the building, the old servants' backstairs takes you to each floor.

As with many old English country homes, the grounds are set in a collection of trees from around the world; the red sequoias were bigger than any tree I had ever seen. The front lawn was the old tennis court, and there was a walled garden at the back of the building.

This grand old house was converted into a boarding school by the Norfolk Education Department as a home for thirty boys.

The national archives (1951) list it as: 'Morley Hall hostel for maladjusted children (senior boys)'.

Wow, maladjusted children. Now, that hurts.

Other descriptions for Morley Hall include: 'home for boys from broken homes' and 'home for older boys with behavioural and learning difficulties'.

The truth is that back in the 1960s to the 1980s, children with ADHD, autism, learning disabilities, dyslexia, and other behavioural problems were left undiagnosed.

Unsure what to do with all the 'problem' children, the Norfolk Education Department would send them all to Morley Hall.

When asked where I went to school, I always tell people I went to a boarding school in Norfolk, and people imagine Eton with nice uniforms, the old school tie, and Harry-Potter hobnobbing with the next prime minister.

Like any other boarding school, the parents and guardians would drop the children off at the start of the school year, and the boys would live there.

Unlike any other boarding school, the Norfolk Education Department had rounded up thirty boys aged twelve to sixteen, whom they had secretly labelled as maladjusted, and put them all in the same place.

The only way this would work was with some discipline and very strict rules.

A BRIEF HISTORY
OF MORLEY HALL

Before we get into the rules of Morley Hall, I wanted to share a brief timeline of the site and some key dates in its history. It's not crucial to the story, so if history is not your thing, you have permission to skip this lesson and move on to the next chapter.

Evidence of pottery kilns and people living on the site that is now Morley Hall dates back to the Roman times around 43AD. Saxon coins and pottery have been found from around 450AD. By 1066, the land was part of the Morley St Peter Manor, and in 1695AD, map evidence shows a boundary along the Morley Estate.

Morley Hall itself was built in 1839 by the Graver Browne family, and, in 1906, it was bought by J. C. Crossley. The estate was put up for sale by auction in 1921, and a golf club was established on the grounds.

From 1939 to 1945, the land was used for wartime food production by local farmer G. L. Peacock, and from 1943 to 1945, the Ministry of Works requisitioned the site for an American Army Hospital to support the nearby bases of the US Army Air Force. After the Second World War, in 1946, the Royal Norfolk Regiment used the site as a transit camp.

The role of Morley Hall as an education establishment started in 1947 when it became a teacher training college. And in 1951, Morley Hall became a boarding school for boys.

After forty-two years, Morley Hall closed its doors for the last time in the spring of 1993. The site was sold by sealed bids and purchased by G.S.D. Lambert & Sons.

View over lawns showing the
East and South Fronts
c. 1920.

View of the front drive c. 1920.

View from the grounds showing
the South-West Aspect c. 1920.

View from park showing the
South Front c. 1920.

RULES AND ROUTINE

Everything at Morley Hall was based on rules and routine. None of them were written down, and you had to learn quickly.

Morley Hall was run by the Norfolk Education Department and managed by the headmaster and his wife, whom the children called Willy and Fanny. They lived on-site in a small cottage and were supported by a team of around ten teachers, sometimes called house parents. As you would at school, you always called them Mr. and Mrs.

Some teachers lived on-site full-time; others did occasional shifts. As in any school, you had the normal mix of characters, from the ones who were kind and caring to the strict ones. Some you could get away with anything, and others you wouldn't dare to do anything wrong.

To keep Morley Hall running with any sense of discipline, the school had a very strict routine, and nothing was optional. You had to be in the right place all the time, and many parts of the building and grounds were out of bounds to the boys.

Every moment of the day was allocated, and you had to stick to it.

A lot of the routine was based on the so-called 'National Service Conscription', which ended in 1963; many of the teachers had experienced this, and it was the template for discipline and order.

Everything was regimented, from the time you got up and had a shower to what you ate and when you ate it, where you would sit, when you could talk and when you had to be silent, going to lessons and doing your homework, the amount of television you could watch and when to go to bed.

You did everything at the same time, and there was no negotiation.

Bad behaviour was not acceptable—no flicking bogies, fighting, or swearing. You had to behave and stick to the rules.

In this book, I hope to share with you the rules. As much as anything, I simply wanted to write them down as nobody ever had.

You might be wondering how I ended up in Morley Hall.

For me, life at home was living with my parents, who frequently screamed, shouted, and threw things at each other.

I spent a lot of time as a little boy sitting on the

stairs, very frightened, and I often ran away from home.

At school, the teachers did not know what to do with me as I appeared both bright and an idiot at the same time.

The problem was that I am dyslexic, something we know about today but not something they understood back then.

And so, the Norfolk County Council Education Department sent me off to Morley Hall.

NUMBERS

Like all institutions, the first thing they do when you arrive is to give you a number. You were allocated the next lowest available number.

I was given the number 'five'.

Everything was done by number, and everything you owned and used had your number on it.

Still today, I think of myself as 'number five'.

STAR SYSTEM

A fter your number, the second biggest thing that would affect everything you did was the star system.

Your number was used for registers and labelling, but your star colour determined who went first in almost everything, the places you could go, and the rooms you could use.

Each week you were allocated a colour based on your behaviour.

Gold – Extremely good
Silver – Very good
Red – Good
Blue – Average
Green – Bad
Yellow – Very Bad
White – Extremely Bad

With each star, you could also be a plus or minus,

so if you behaved well but not well enough to be promoted, you might get a 'plus' to indicate you were moving in the right direction.

Equally, if you had not behaved well, you might get a minus as a warning.

Once a week, the teachers would have a meeting to discuss the boy's behaviour and assign your star.

On Friday after teatime, the star colours would be announced; either the headmaster or lead teacher would read out each person's number and tell you what star you would have for the week.

With each colour came a different level of freedom, restrictions, reward, and punishment.

Gold Star

You had to do something extraordinary for this status. Each term, maybe one boy would get the gold star status for a week or so. It was only ever given in very special circumstances. With the gold star status, you got the first choice on everything and could even use the main grand staircase, usually reserved for staff only and strictly out of bounds for the boys.

Silver Star

This was very special. Very few people made it to the silver star status; with a silver star, you could access the 'silver room', which was on the first floor of the house and had a television, kettle, and a toaster. It was a very special treat as nobody else could even make a cup of tea. You could access this room during free time, and only boys with a silver star could enter the room; you were even given your own key for the door. Normally only a couple of silver stars would be awarded any week.

Red Star

If you were good, you might be awarded a red star. This would give you access to the 'red room'; this was a nice room on the ground floor with some comfortable seating and games. You could also go to parts of the ground normally out of bounds. Normally no more than five of the boys would be a red star at any time.

Blue Star

To be fair, everybody started as a blue star, and this was generally where most people would stay. You did not get any special treatment or any restrictions.

Green Star

Any boy causing trouble or not following the rules would be made a green star. You would be one of the last in line when things got selected. Some boys were just always causing trouble, and so they remained a green star.

Yellow Star

If you just kept causing trouble or did something really bad, then you would be a yellow star. You now had to always stay in sight of the building so a teacher could see you. It was not often boys were a yellow star.

White Star
This was reserved for real trouble like running away or causing criminal damage or theft. You had to be in your pyjamas at all times, and your clothes would be locked away.

At the start of each term, everybody would be a blue star, so everyone had the chance to make a fresh start.

Some boys were naturally better-behaved than others, and you knew who was going to be bad and get a lower star and who was going to be good and get a higher one.

But there was also a third category: Some boys were very skilled at manipulating the situation and could be very badly behaved, but very good at fooling the system and getting away with making trouble while getting rewarded at the same time.

THE SQUARE

I t was the simplest punishment and the most common. As you entered Morley Hall, the hallway itself had a tile floor made up of bright red and yellow colours in the shape of three squares equally spaced along the corridor diagonally. Each square was around one metre in length on each side, and the coloured tiles were boarded with some plain cream ones to clearly mark each one.

They were called 'the square'.

If you did something wrong, you were sent to the square.

You might have spoken when you should have been quiet, back-chatted a teacher, or just generally misbehaved. It would not take much to be punished.

Once on the square, you were not allowed to move, talk, or sit down. The length of time you stayed on the square would depend on what you had done and the teacher's mood.

Some teachers would love sending people to the square for anything at all or nothing. They would have the power to keep you on the square for as long as they wanted.

Most of the time, the square was used as a place to cool down following an altercation or at the first sign of trouble.

If you were sent at night, the floor was cold and the hallway dark; it was not very pleasant.

Too many trips to the square would be noticed, and you would be dropping a star as punishment by Friday.

LINES

A common punishment in all schools and one loved by teachers is doing lines. Writing the same phrase over and over for as many times as the teacher demanded.

A favourite at Morley Hall, as it is still all around the world. You would be sent to the dining room with a sheet of paper and could not leave until they were all completed.

I knew one of the boys who had a great technique of holding several pens at the same time to get them done quicker.

PINNED DOWN

S ometimes things just got out of hand, and all the shouting and sending to the square was simply not enough. If you got into a fight, tantrum, or things got physical, you would get pinned down by one of the teachers.

The aim was physical restraint to stop you from hurting yourself or somebody else. First, they would pull your legs away from underneath you, and you would fall to the ground, put their knee on your back and, with their hand, hold your head face-down until you calmed down.

Sometimes boys were just looking for a fight, and it was inevitable that this would be the result.

It was always the same teachers who wanted to use this technique; they liked to show who was boss with overwhelming force and sometimes seemed to enjoy the confrontation.

Some teachers simply never got aggressive like

this with the boys and found other ways to control bad behaviour.

HEADMASTER'S OFFICE

As you entered Morley Hall, the headmaster's office was the first room on the right. You did not want to find yourself being sent to see the headmaster; this only happened when things went so wrong the teacher had run out of options.

The room was full of the history of Morley Hall and not just the school. I remember old wooden tennis rackets that looked Victorian in a square racket press, wood and glass cabinets filled with items that had been collected, and metal filing cabinets of different sizes lined the room.

His large wooden desk was facing the door, and the room was built around it. In front of the desk was a chair, and you would only sit down if told to.

The phone was the rotary style one in dark olive

green where you had a wheel move the numbers around.

At a time before computers were common, the headmaster had an Amstrad word processor that displayed the text in green on a black screen and was very high-tech for the day.

PERSONAL
RECORD

Locked away in a filing cabinet in the headmaster's office were the personal records for each boy. What was in the records was a subject of much speculation; we knew they existed but had never seen them.

Unlike a prison or Borstal, you had not been sentenced to spend time at Morley Hall, and the reason for your stay was often unclear.

'Why are you here?' was a common question boys would ask each other. Some would have a clear answer as they had done something at school that resulted in them being expelled or a series of behavioural problems like causing trouble, running away, or fighting.

Often, the boys just didn't know the answer to that question, and a little look into their records to find out what had been said about them was something they all desperately wanted.

Looking back now, it's clear that many of the boys just had behavioural issues that today would have been identified and dealt with differently.

Now, I find myself curious once again about what the records might have said, so I submitted a 'Subject Access Request' to the Norfolk County Council.

Sadly, they found nothing in the records or with the Norfolk government archives. Under Morley Hall, it reads: 'It is mentioned in the Norfolk education committee's report, Education in Norfolk, 1950–1960, but there are no records of this school deposited with us'.

CORPORAL PUNISHMENT

It was not until 1986 that corporal punishment was banned in UK schools. The threat of the cane, a slipper, or a hand hitting you was something the headmaster would have used as a last resort.

This was not common—maybe once a year, this would happen, and it would be the headmaster who did the actual punishment.

Normally it would be a slipper. The cane, however, was displayed in the office; I never knew of it being used on anybody. I think it was more for show—as a deterrent or maybe a souvenir of days gone.

If the situation had got so bad you were going to be hit with the slipper, things must have gone terribly wrong.

This would be for serious damage to people's property or an individual, something one step removed from seeing the police.

One weekend, a couple of the boys left the grounds without permission and went down to the farmer's field, where they smashed the glass dials on a tractor. The farmer had seen the boys and angrily made his way to Morley Hall.

All the boys were called into the television room and the farmer, who looked very angry, gave us a lecture about how much the damage would cost him.

That night, the two boys who were responsible were given the slipper by the headmaster.

GRASS

L ike in any institution, the rules were not just made by the teachers; the boys had a code too.

As with any good prison drama, the first rule was no grassing.

You might not be familiar with the term 'grass' other than a nice green lawn; it means to snitch, rat, tell, blab, talk, or tell somebody in authority about somebody else who has broken the rules.

It is not clear where the word comes from, and it is a very English saying. Maybe rhyming slang for 'copper' (the nickname for a police officer) would be 'grasshopper' and so 'grass?'

If you 'shop' somebody, you have told the police, and so maybe 'grasshopper' is from 'grass-shopper?' We will never actually know.

But what is very clear is that nobody likes a 'grass', and it was not tolerated.

Should you be found to be a 'grass', the boys would not talk to you or include you in anything, and heated shouts of 'grass' would be aimed at you.

A teacher might find some damage that had been done by one of the boys, but they wouldn't know who had done it.

To find out, everybody would be put together in a room and told that nobody would leave until somebody admitted it.

This never worked.

If anybody talked, they would be in a lot of trouble with the other boys, so the room would remain very silent for a long time.

Normally, somebody innocent would be the fall guy and just admit to doing it to break the deadlock so everybody could move on.

BEASTING

If you annoyed the other boys by grassing on somebody or just being irritating, you might be subject to a beasting.

Normally quite mild and harmless, but it made the point that you needed to get in line and remember which team you were on.

Unlike its name, a beasting does not mean being beaten up or anything physical. Okay, you might get a dead-arm, Chinese burn, or be held under a mattress while everybody laid a punch on you.

More often, you will find the bed you had just made stripped or your things on the floor, your towel might go missing, or your bed given an apple turnover—this is where the bottom sheet of the bed is folded back up so when you get in, you can only get halfway down.

During shower time, you might get a towel snapping; this is where a wet towel is twisted around itself to make it like a whip and then flicked. And when you are wet from just getting out of the shower in the winter, that really hurts.

Anything more than a mild beasting was soon put down. As you can imagine, things could get heated, and arguments could soon move to squabbles and fighting, but an actual fight was not common, and the teachers soon dealt with any situation.

FIRE DRILL

E ach term, the fire evacuation plan had to be tested, and the fire drill was something to look forward to.

As with any group of young boys, playing around with fire and fire alarms was great fun. The teachers would do anything to ensure neither was available to play with.

All matches and lighters were banned; however, many of the older boys smoked, and cigarettes, lighters, and matches were well hidden around the house and grounds.

A fire drill was normally practiced during the night in the middle of the week, sometime after all the boys were asleep around 10PM or 11PM.

The fire alarm was loud. Very loud.

Across the building were multiple sirens and bells installed at different times, and the combined sound could be heard everywhere.

Before you went to bed, you had to make your clothes into a bundle; you would lay out your trousers and then lay on top of them all your clothes and then roll them up into a 'bundle'.

When the fire alarm sounded, you would put on your shoes, grab your bundle, and make your way out of the building; a teacher would be at each point along the route.

From your bedroom, you would make your way down the main staff staircase (normally out of bounds for the boys).

At the bottom of the stairs, you would make a left onto the long corridor, through the main entrance (also normally out of bounds for the boys), and then onto the gravel drive outside.

The cold night air would hit you as you would be in your pyjamas, and this was the point at which you would realise if you had forgotten to put your shoes on in all the confusion as the stones would hurt your feet.

The route continued around the drive to the back of the building and the old courtyard; this was a large square made from small black cobbles directly outside the old stables now used for storage.

Each boy would stand on the edge and form a line around the perimeter of the square. When everybody was out of the building, they would take the register.

You would line up in number order, and when told to start, the first boy would shout 'one', then this would continue down the line.

Often a number would be missing as a boy had left and the number was not yet allocated, and so it was not a complete set of numbers from one to thirty.

This would often cause the problem of somebody saying the wrong number and just saying the next number by mistake instead of their number.

If this happened, we would do it again until we got it right.

Sometimes, one of the boys would deliberately make a mistake, and it would keep going for a few rounds. During a fire drill at 11PM, they couldn't send you back into the 'burning' building to stand on the square; it was just a bit of fun.

The teachers would have a coat, and so they would play the power game back and just keep you standing outside for longer. Eventually, the boys would give in and get the numbers right.

Then, it was back into Morley Hall via the normal boy's entrance at the back of the building, up the old servant's staircase and back to bed.

Nobody could sleep through the noise and commotion, given how loud the alarms were and with everybody running around.

However, one night as the boys made a line around the square in the courtyard, the teacher started the count...

'One, two, three, four... six... Stop, where is number five?'

I was fast asleep in bed still.

For some reason, I just didn't wake up that night, and in the rush to get out, everybody just missed me, and I stayed asleep.

One of the teachers came and gently woke me up and whispered that it was a fire drill.

Once I was fully awake, the shouting started...

'GET UP, and GET OUT NOW!'

Finally, I arrived at the courtyard to a raucous welcome of clapping and gearing as nobody could believe I had slept through it all.

THE BELL

The grounds of Morley Hall were very large. You had multiple lawns, woods, fields, gardens, and places to play outside; the building was big enough to get very lost in, and so they needed a way to call you back.

When the building was an old English country house, they used a gong to let people know when food was served. The old gong was still to be found at the bottom of the grand staircase, but now it was strictly forbidden to touch it.

The same system that they used for the fire alarm could be used as a bell. In the kitchen was the magic button, and a quick press would sound the alarm across the building; this could be heard right across the grounds.

When the bell sounded, you knew it was time to report back.

Occasionally, you might be asked to press the

button. As it was in the kitchen, it was already out of bounds.

You never touched the button without permission; I don't ever remember any of the boys touching it unless they were told to do so.

SCHOOL
MINIBUS

Every school has a minibus; I see them today with their logos and names proudly written down the side and smile. The last thing Morley Hall wanted to do was warn people that the Morley Hall Boys had arrived by putting our name on the bus, and we definitely didn't have a school logo.

The bus was old and had been handed down from another school that had purchased a new one. It had no heater or air conditioning, so it was freezing in the winter and baking hot in the summer.

In the back sat a basic wooden bench bolted to the floor and no seatbelts; if the driver braked too hard, we would all end up at the front of the bus.

It was very old and rusty, and the door locks

were broken, not that anybody would have wanted
to steal it anyway.

HOME
WEEKENDS &
TERM END

M orley Hall was your home for the school term, and you went home during the school holidays. If you didn't have a home to go to, you might go to foster parents or other guardians.

When you are twelve, the school term feels very long.

Some weekends were designated as 'home weekends'; they were normally during the longer terms to give the boys a chance to go home.

If you were lucky, your parents would pick you up from Morley Hall. Else it was the school minibus ride from hell, taking what felt like hours going round all of Norfolk.

The school would run the minibus to Norwich, then across to East Dereham, Swaffham, and King's Lynn to drop the boys off at home, bus stations, train stations, pick-up points, and countless stops.

Some boys didn't go home for the weekends—not many, normally no more than five.

For some, this was a choice; they wanted to stay. Maybe their home was not a nice place to go back to. For others, it was a chance to have Morley Hall to themselves.

Staying over at 'home weekend' was special; you had more freedom to do your own thing and have all the grounds to play in.

Usually, just one teacher would stay behind to look after the few that were left, so you could build a better relationship with them.

RUNNING AWAY

Normally, once a term, one of the boys would just snap and do a runner.

Morley Hall itself was surrounded by trees and farmland, so you didn't have anywhere to go that was close.

The nearest village is Morley St. Peter, but it's just a few houses with a small shop and the closest towns are Attleborough and Wymondham. Both are going to take an hour to walk, and Norwich would be more than four hours away.

If you did a runner, you would need to get the timing right. With so much of your day timetabled, people would quickly notice you were missing.

Somebody looking for a better star next week was going to grass you up if they saw you, so you needed to be very secretive.

Morley Hall is in the very centre of the grounds

of Wymondham College. The drive is a mile long from end to end, so you are already surrounded by teachers and in a very exposed place.

The chances of making it out of the grounds without being seen were slim.

Once somebody was reported missing, the bell was sounded to call all the boys back to the television room and then the teachers would try to find out information, and the search would be on.

Most runaways would be rounded up very quickly and returned.

As punishment, you would immediately be demoted to a white star, have your clothes and shoes confiscated, and remain in your pyjamas and slippers for a week.

All the boys would ask the same question: 'How far did you get?'

It was as if the boys had never been allowed out of Morley Hall ever and were desperate for news beyond the wall. The story of the runaway would be something shared with friends and enjoyed like an adventure around the world.

However, to be a successful runaway, you had to be smart.

Occasionally, we would be allowed a minibus trip out of the grounds at the weekend.

To be allowed on a trip out, you would need to be at least a blue star, and the chances are if you were looking to do a runner, you would already be a green star or below.

But every so often, one of the boys on the trip

out made a run for it.

This was your best chance of getting away as you were already far from Morley Hall, and you would only have one teacher looking after you, maybe two at the very most.

Once let out of the minibus, you would need to choose the people you were going to be with carefully. Any little whispers of running would soon be picked up, and somebody might grass to try and get a better star next week, so you had to keep quiet. Also, the person you were with was at risk of being punished for not saying anything, so they needed to leave it as long as they could before reporting you missing. Then you had the best chance of escape, and they had the best chance of not getting punished.

This was the worst situation for the teacher who had taken you out for the day. Now, they were on their own with no support to find the runaway and still had a bus full of boys to take care of.

The best they could do was get everybody back on the bus and get as much information as possible. Nobody was going to say anything and be a grass in front of everybody else; if somebody knew anything, they might tell quietly.

It was now a case of driving about and looking around the streets.

The teacher's advantage was a minibus with good height and a bus full of spotters; the runaway was alone, but they could quickly hide, and the minibus was not exactly the best covert undercover vehicle.

If the runaway was not found, then the bus had to return to Morley Hall with one less passenger.

The teacher was now in a very difficult situation; they had to report to the headmaster that they had lost one of the boys and couldn't find them.

The boys, however, had a very exciting story to tell of how one of them had done a runner.

The police would be called, and normally the escapee would be found quickly and returned to tell the tale of their day on the run.

I remember returning on a trip from Wicklewood, a small village near Morley Hall. The route back takes you across some fields with a single-track roadway. The start of the road is on a small hill, and it had become something of a tradition to play a little game with the minibus and one of the boys.

At the top of the road, the minibus would park and switch off the engine; the runner would set off down the road on foot and then the bus would release the handbrake and roll down the hill. If the runner made it first, they would be the winner!

This was always very exciting, our own Olympic event. As you would expect, the bus made a slow start while the runner made good ground. Normally, around two-thirds of the way down, the bus would catch the runner, who would be quite exhausted by then.

But this time was different.

In a stroke of genius by one of the boys, he had persuaded the teacher to let him play the game and was let out of the bus. As expected, he got a good head start and made a run for it.

The bus rolled down the hill, and as we got to the bottom, the boy was nowhere to be seen.

As the road turned behind a hedge, he had hidden in a ditch, and the bus rolled past. He then doubled back and was on the run.

At the bottom of the hill, we were all looking around and waiting for him to jump out and claim victory, but nothing; he was nowhere to be seen, and it took a moment for everybody to understand what had happened.

The bus quickly turned around, and the search was on, but it was just too late, and he was gone.

Now, this was a great game we played with a few of the teachers; it was not exactly official or endorsed by the headmaster.

We had to return to Morley Hall, and the teacher had to explain that he had lost one of the boys.

But worse, he had to explain that he gave him a good head start and told him to start running. It was one of the few occasions the teacher was in more trouble than any of the boys.

As you can expect, our little game was now banned.

MY TIME ON
THE RUN

Now, it was my turn to make a run for it.

I was normally well behaved with a blue star, frequently red and occasionally even a silver, and if you asked all the boys who was likely to do a runner, my name would not have come up.

After being sent to Morley Hall, the fighting continued at home, and every few months during school holidays, I got home and saw what was happening.

With the short holidays and long terms, I only got to experience little bits every few months. I think this made it worse. Rather than living with it, you got dropped in and then taken away again.

Inevitably, my parents divorced, and one day, I found myself standing in a courtroom with people in suits all trying to explain to me that I was now a 'ward of the court'.

'A child under the supervision of and protected under the inherent jurisdiction of the High Court. When a child is made a ward of the court, responsibility for him or her is vested in the court, although day-to-day care and control may rest with an individual or a local authority'.

For the next few years, along with being at Morley Hall during the school terms, I would spend school holidays with a mixture of foster parents or with either my mum or dad.

One day at school, I got asked to go to the headmaster's office. The head was looking very serious and asked me to sit down. You never get asked to sit down in the office; you only ever get asked in the office if you have done something wrong and never to sit.

He told me that my dad had had a serious stroke and was unwell.

A few weeks later, my dad was able to visit me at Morley Hall. The door opened, and I saw him for the first time in a wheelchair. He was clearly unwell and unable to move or talk properly.

For the first time in my life, I fell backwards, like I had actually been knocked back. I don't think the shock ever left me.

One night, at around 11PM, I got out of bed, put the covers back neatly, quietly collected my bundle, picked up my shoes, and then crept down the main staff staircase. I opened the two main doors that were locked with a small yale latch, and I locked the latch open so as not to cause a loud click as it closed.

I got dressed, put on my shoes, and was on the run.

The back drive had more tree cover than the front drive; however, it was the back of Wymondham College, and you risked being seen by their teachers or students who would raise the alarm, so I headed down the front drive.

Out of the grounds, I made it down to the main road and walked along the roadside as far as I could, past Attleborough, towards Snetterton, and then on the way to Thetford.

My aim was to get to Suffolk and Bury St. Edmunds; I knew somebody very kind who lived there, and I was now well on the way.

Just outside Attleborough, I tried to hitch a ride; it was cold and dark and not easy for the cars to see me. Eventually, the draft from a large lorry knocked me off my feet into a ditch. Exhausted, I fell asleep on the side of the road.

The next day, I woke up to a much better situation; you could clearly see the cars, and they could see you.

It was not long before a car stopped just outside Snetterton, and I had finally managed to get a lift. A nice man asked where I was going and kindly agreed to help take me along the way.

I was in a nice warm car and making very good progress.

Seeing the sign for Thetford, I knew I had done well—now almost out of Norfolk and into Suffolk.

As we drove down Norwich Road through the town, the man said he wanted to make a quick stop and pulled over.

As I looked out of the window, I saw the police station sign. I knew it was over.

Hungry, tired, and exhausted, I knew running was not an option. The man kindly explained that it was not safe to be running away and took me to the police station.

I was really upset to have not made it to Bury St. Edmunds. Looking back now, I was lucky to have been picked up and taken to the police station.

The police are not really equipped to deal with runaway boys; the sergeant got me a cup of tea and a plaster for some blisters on my feet.

Not taking any chances, they put me in a cell and locked the door. The large metal door crashed closed with the distinctive sound of metal-on-metal echoing in a room with no furniture.

I don't know how long I was in the cell for before I was collected by the headmaster. He told me that he knew something was wrong as soon as he got up as I had left the door on the latch.

The trip back was very quiet, and when I arrived at Morley Hall, I knew what I had to do, something I had seen many times. I went up to the bedrooms, got my pyjamas and slippers, and handed in my normal clothes.

Sitting in the television room on the ground

floor, I waited. Eventually, I was called into the headmaster's office. He kindly let me use the telephone to call the person I was going to see.

I was demoted to a white star but quickly made my way back to blue over the next couple of weeks.

My dad died that summer.

MATRON

The headmaster's wife was the school matron and dealt with any boys who were sick or unwell. Getting a day off school because you were ill was almost impossible. They knew every trick in the book, and you stood no chance of getting away with it.

If you claimed to have a temperature or were feeling unwell, out would come the glass thermometer, and placed under your tongue for a couple of minutes and then back to the matron for inspection.

This was normally done at breakfast. Unless you were almost dead, you still had to get up and dressed before being checked. This way, you were almost out of the door for school.

The problem with this plan for the matron was that the breakfast table was full of hot things to put the thermometer on to get a fake high temperature.

However, getting the thermometer to read something higher than normal without going too high was very difficult.

Putting the thermometer on the teapot was popular, as was dipping it in your tea. I remember one boy putting the thermometer in his cup, and the mercury expanded so much that it broke the end of the thermometer into his tea along with all the mercury.

As the matron returned to check his thermometer, he quickly put it back in his mouth without noticing. On removing the thermometer, he soon got busted and sent to school—without his cup of tea.

At the start of one term, I arrived back at Morley Hall not feeling well after the long car journey and too many chips for my tea. At suppertime, in the dining room, I started to be sick and was sent to the bathrooms, leaving a trail of sick all the way down the corridor.

Being ill was never encouraged, and the teacher told me off for eating too many chips and gave me a mop to clean up the mess I had made.

MARGARET THATCHER'S TOILET

In January 1974, the education secretary Margaret Thatcher visited schools in Norfolk, including Morley Hall.

It was well before my time at the school, but the visit left Morley Hall with an unusual claim to fame that the matron was very keen to tell people about.

While visiting the school, Margaret Thatcher was taken short and asked to use the toilet facilities. The nearest one was a very old 'WC' with a big water tank on the top, a grand ceramic base, and a pull handle.

No longer used as a toilet in the 80s—but very proudly, any visitor would be taken to the closet and shown the toilet that the then-current prime minister had once used back in 1974.

STORM 1987

The great storm of 1987 was a cyclone causing massive damage across the south and east of England, and Morley Hall was right in its path.

That night, the storm hit in the early morning hours, and trees all over the grounds fell.

The electricity was cut off, and the emergency back-up lighting kicked in. It was like a disaster zone across the grounds, and, as with any break in the routine, it caused much excitement.

I would like to tell a tale of a night in total terror as we worried about the storm hitting us, the trees taking out the house, and the wind so strong it ripped the tiles off the roof, and we watched them fly across the grounds. However, as with the fire alarm, I slept through it all—again.

In the morning, we had no power at all, and the site was blocked on both drives as so many trees had fallen and no vehicles could get to us.

The local timber merchant from the village was called to bring chainsaws, and it took them until lunchtime to cut an access path back to the house.

At the front of the site on the longer drive, it would take them until the end of the year before access was restored as so many big trees blocked the road.

The two grand sequoia trees survived the storm; if they had fallen, they were big enough to hit the house. Eventually, in another storm, one did fall and left a permanent dent in the lawn that could never be removed.

BILLY GRAHAM

American evangelist and ordained Southern Baptist minister Billy Graham toured the world preaching to huge stadiums and made a trip to Carrow Road football stadium in Norwich in 1984.

His tour of the UK was a massive event leading the news, and he filled stadiums with his American evangelist-style preaching, never seen before in the UK.

A small group of boys were allowed to visit Carrow Road and see Billy Graham preach, and I was lucky enough to be selected.

Most of the boys were not religious, but this was an escape from the school and to a massive stadium with thousands of people, so the trip had many volunteers wanting to go.

At the end of the meeting, Billy Graham invited people down to the pitch to accept Jesus into their lives.

However, when people got to the bottom of the stairs, they were prevented from going on the grass itself. It's rumoured that the head groundsman said, 'Not on my pitch, they're not'.

We were not allowed on the grass, and the quote is part of the folklore of the event.

After the event, we were treated to fish and chips in Wymondham on the way back to the hall.

THE GHOST OF
MORLEY HALL

E very old house needs a ghost story, and Morley Hall is no exception to the rule. With thirty boys and creative imaginations, you would expect lots of them.

But the ghost story of Morley Hall is not from the boys; it has been passed down through the generations of staff working at the hall and is well documented.

The story of the ghost of the Scottie Dog of Morley Hall dates back to when the house was in private use as a home by a wealthy industrialist who had one son. On the boy's twenty-first birthday, he was given a puppy Scottish Terrier dog he named 'Scottie'.

Soon after, the boy went away to college, and the puppy was looked after by the coachman who lived in the cottage at the back of Morley Hall. In the 80s, this was the home of the headmaster and his wife.

After the son returned from college, he started a relationship with one of the servant girls who became pregnant. When the boy's father found out, the son denied the relationship and the girl was dismissed. Her parents took them to court, but they lost the case.

The shame was too much for the boy, and days after the court hearing, he shot the dog and himself.

On the grounds of Morley Hall is a little pet cemetery with small gravestones. Still there today is a little headstone with the name 'Scottie' on it, where the coachman had once buried him.

Today, Scottie still walks the grounds of Morley Hall as a little ghost dog.

The first record of Scottie being seen as a ghost comes from the cook's assistant back in the 1950s, and many other members of staff have witnessed the little dog. He is described as a little black Scottie dog with a blue glow and wearing a braided leather tartan collar. The little dog would run into rooms and simply disappear again.

From the kitchen, the cook's assistant would have a clear view of the courtyard, and when Scottie appeared, she would call out, 'There is that little dog again'.

Reports also came from other members of staff in the years that followed, including the groundsman and the matron, who also saw the little dog walking around the grounds, up the stairs, and into rooms—as large as life and leaving them unsure if it was an actual dog or the ghost of Scottie.

DINING-ROOM
ETIQUETTE

O f all the rules at Morley Hall, the dining room was the one place with the most. Like any family, the dining room was the place with the most opportunities for things to go wrong with arguments and disagreements.

The dining room was at the end of the ground floor of the building and 35ft by 18ft (10m x 5.5m). It had two entrances and large windows the size of doors going down the room's length, each with huge Victorian shutters. The end of the room was a large semicircle with doors opening out into the grounds.

In the room were seven dining tables, each with five or six chairs. The head of the table would have a chair with arms and was reserved for the teacher. If the school was busy, you might have thirty or thirty-three boys and six teachers altogether.

It was a grand room with tall ceilings and a large wooden cupboard for storing plates and cutlery, and above the fireplace was a strange set of cow horns with a little tuft of hair in the centre.

At the start of each term, you could choose the table you wanted to sit on. The boys would line up outside and wait their turn to enter the room and select a chair.

You wanted to sit with your friends, and so the race was on to ensure you got the place you wanted. Equally, some boys were not popular, and you didn't want them at your table.

The order you went in to select your place was a little more random. Normally, the star system would sort out the order; however, at the beginning of term, everybody got reset back to a blue star.

They could just use the number system, but then you would always have the lower numbers choosing the best places.

If you just sent everybody in at the same time, it would have been more like Black Friday in Oxford Circus.

Depending on the teacher, it would either be by star average, your number, or random order.

Once you have been released into the room, you'd want the place at the top left of the table as the top right was the server, and nobody liked that job. Each week, you would move around one place to the left, and so if the term was more than five weeks, you could end up being the server twice.

The tables would start to build with each boy that entered the room. Even if you were next in, you might not get the place you wanted to sit.

Reserving a seat was strictly forbidden, but the boys who were green, yellow, and white stars were often that colour for a reason and usually the ones happier to pick a fight, so if you selected a table and a chair that was reserved, the other boys would tell you to move on and get lost. If you didn't, you would pay for the rest of the term.

Being a higher star could also have its problems. If you went in early and selected an empty table, others might not sit with you, and then you could end up with a table full of boys nobody wanted to sit with, and mealtimes might not be very nice.

When you entered the dining room for meals, you had to stand behind your chair until everybody else had arrived, and then the teacher would give permission to sit down.

Once you were in the dining room, it was strict silence until everybody was served—no talking or making any noise at all.

If you broke the rules when in the dining room, you would be asked to stand behind your chair. If this happened, you were not allowed to eat or drink until you were asked to sit back down. You could miss a part of the meal when this happened; normally, the punishment was for just a short time, and they never actually made you miss a whole meal.

A hot teaspoon in the back of another boy's hand was a common trick in the dining room. You put your teaspoon in a cup of tea or on the side of a teapot to get it hot, then quickly onto another boy's hand and then wait for the shouting. Either they got asked to stand up for making a noise, or you did for making it happen, or both of you for disrupting the room.

During meals, standing behind your chair was more favourable to the teachers than the square. If they sent you out of the room to the square, then they couldn't see you, and all the teachers would be in the dining room. Better to have you in sight where they could see what you were doing.

If you learned nothing else from your time at Morley Hall, then table manners were something no boy left without understanding.

Every meal was in the dining room, and you only had the food that was given at the time it was served. If you didn't eat it, you didn't eat.

Each day, we would be in the dining room for breakfast, dinner, teatime, and supper.

Once everybody sat down, it was the server's job to get the food from the kitchen. Each server would make their way into the kitchen next to the dining room and collect two plates at a time. The kitchen staff would serve up the meals equally in the kitchen, ready for collection.

Once everybody was served, it was time for grace. Normally, this was said by one of the boys at the selection of the head teacher, and everybody was expected to bow their head in silence.

'For what we are about to receive, may the Lord make us truly thankful'. Everybody would then say 'amen' and be allowed to start eating and talking.

You had to use your knife and fork properly, and they had to be held correctly by the handle between the thumb and forefinger. Both had to be held, and you were not allowed to put either one down while eating. The knife was only to be used for cutting the food. You were never to put the knife anywhere near your mouth and never lick it under any circumstances. Your fork was to be used the correct way up, and if you used it upside down, somebody would let you know 'it was a fork and not a shovel', and yes, that included eating peas.

With desserts, you would have a spoon and a fork. The spoon was used for eating the food, and the fork to help cut and put the food on the spoon.

Under no circumstances were you to put your elbows on the table. If you did, they would get whacked by the heavy end of a knife, this really hurt, and you'd never forget that rule again.

Drinks were served in cups, and you had to hold them by the handle. Shouts of 'that cup has a handle, so use it' would be the response if you forgot.

No slouching in your chair or on the table; you would sit up straight.

You were allowed to talk during the meal to people at your own table, never to other tables, between courses, and absolutely never with food in your mouth.

Eating with your mouth open was also quickly addressed, again with a quick shout of 'don't eat with your mouth open'.

Each course would be served, and you were not allowed to start until everybody at your table was served, and everybody was seated and ready.

You didn't have to take the food being offered, but you did have to eat the food you took.

Once you finished, your knife and fork had to be placed together side by side on the plate neatly.

At the end of each course, you had to pass your plates around the table from left to right so the server could stack all the plates on top of each other with the cutlery on top and then make one trip to the kitchen with them.

Discipline in the dining room was very strict; if you didn't comply, you would be standing behind your chair watching everybody else eat. You'd soon fall in line with the rules or go hungry.

One breakfast, the headmaster arrived after a rather brutal haircut. One of the louder tables decided to start chanting, 'Willy has had a haircut', louder and louder. The headmaster was not impressed and confiscated the teapot leaving just water for breakfast.

During one teatime, another boy knocked my cup of tea over my cake. I was not impressed and refused to eat the tea-soaked sponge. The teacher wouldn't accept the excuse and said the cake must be eaten, but I still refused. I was told to stand behind my chair until I was ready to eat it. Everybody else continued, and all the plates were cleared except mine.

Now in a classic stand-off, nobody was allowed to leave the room until I had finished. And I was never going to be eating the wet cake and drinking the now cold tea.

We waited for a long time with a lot of restlessness from the rest of the room. Lots of the boys made comments and were unhappy to be stuck in the room.

Eventually, the teacher gave in, and everybody was released. But this was not over yet; I would be given that piece of cake and cold tea for every meal until it was gone.

The kitchen staff were on my side and threw away the tea and left the cake to dry. By the next meal, I gave in and ate the cake.

Even now, I struggle not to say anything when I see people with their elbows on the dining table, and if I use a fork upside down to pick up some peas, I catch myself looking around to see if anybody has noticed.

If 'manners make the man', then every boy left Morley Hall equipped to be a man.

PAYPHONE & LETTERS

It was the 1980s and well before anybody started using mobile phones, emails, social media, or laptop computers.

The school had one payphone the boys could use; it was outside the dining room just before the kitchen, and you could use it after homework and before supper for a couple of hours.

People could phone you, and then, if you were lucky, somebody would answer the phone and take the time to look around for you.

The best plan was to agree a time in advance, so you knew they were calling, and you could wait by the phone to answer it.

It was a pay phone taking either a 5p or 10p coin, and the school didn't give out change, so you had to have the money ready.

The phone had a small round booth on the top for some privacy, but anybody could listen in on your call; it was not exactly discreet.

Some people would write letters. It was always nice to get a letter from home, and some boys would get a lot of post from family.

PERSONAL BOX

Most items could be kept in your bedside drawer, but anything of value should be in your personal box. This was a small room at the end of the house between the kitchen and dining room, just opposite the payphone.

It was a small square room with a large door; the door itself was about the size of the room. It was previously used as a safe.

Around the three sides of the room were thirty boxes, all numbered, one for each boy.

The room was locked, and you could only ask to get to your box after homework and before supper.

The boxes were cardboard filing boxes, like a small magazine file or storage box, about the size of a ream of paper.

It was the best place to keep anything you didn't want to go missing or get lost. To get access, you had to persuade a teacher to unlock the door; if they were busy, it might take some time to get it opened.

A DAY AT
MORLEY HALL

The morning would start with a teacher opening the bedroom door and letting you know it was time to get up, normally rather loudly, shouting something like 'get out of your pits'. The curtains and window would be opened, and you knew it was time to move.

They went from one end of the floor to another and then back again. If you were still in bed after that, then it was trouble. The teacher would just pull your bedding off the bed and throw it across the room, which was normally the end of it.

Anybody who kept refusing or was a regular offender was at risk of being tipped.

Tipping was very simple and effective. The teacher would simply lift and tip over your bed— all of it, the bedding, mattress, and frame—and all with you in it.

Some teachers liked to do this, and depending on who was on that morning, you might change your mind about how fast you got up. Other boys would be happy to help too, and some were very keen for an order from the teacher to tip some beds for them.

WASH TIME

Each morning you had a strip wash in the sinks, you would collect your towel, which was on a hook in the bathroom. Each towel and hook was numbered, so you knew which one was yours.

Wrapping your towel around you and using a face cloth, you would have a wash in the sinks.

With just three or four sinks and around ten or fifteen boys on each floor, you had to wait your turn.

The teacher would provide you with the toothpaste and sometimes check if your toothbrush was wet and whether you had cleaned your teeth.

GETTING DRESSED

In each room was a wardrobe with your clothes, just the ones you were using as everything else was stored away, so nothing got lost.

In the mornings, you would put on your school uniform and then hang up your play clothes. Your uniform always had to be perfect and neat, with your shirt done up to the very top button and your tie with a fresh knot every morning.

In the 80s, school children were rebelling against the kipper ties of the 70s and would have their ties backwards with the thin back section on the front. This was not allowed at Morley Hall, so you would do your tie twice, once at Morley Hall and then again on the way to school to switch it around.

MAKING YOUR BED

One of the most important rules at Morley Hall was making your bed properly. The teacher would inspect your bed, and if it was not right, then you would be told to do it again. If they were in a bad mood, it was likely to be stripped by the teacher and thrown around the room.

Each bed has two sheets, a blanket and a top cover. The sheets and blankets were issued by the Norfolk County Council to schools, hospitals, and other institutions. All the same, and none of them new.

To make your bed correctly, you placed the first sheet on the bed with equal material on all sides and then tucked in the sheet under the mattress with hospital corners on all four sides. If you don't know how to do hospital corners, it's not easy to explain—a bit like wrapping a present, the corners of the bed have a perfectly straight fold. Anything less was getting stripped. All boys would need to become experts at making beds with hospital corners.

Next, the second sheet was added, but you only tucked in the base and sides, not the top, again with hospital corners, please.

Now you could add the blanket, and again, just tuck in the base with hospital corners and not the top. You now turned down the top sheet and blanket, so you had a fold showing around 1ft (30cm) of sheet over the folded blanket at the top of the bed, leaving enough space for a pillow.

The sides were now tucked in all the way straight under the bed to the length of the material. It should be as neat under the bed as on the top. The opening at the top should feel tight, and everything should be neat and tidy.

Finally, you would add the pillow, ensuring the pillowcase's opening was facing away from the door and your pyjamas neatly folded under, then you'd add the top cover over everything, ensuring the sides were of equal length.

Once you were ready, you could then get the teacher to inspect your bed for approval.

The teacher needed to get your floor up, washed, dressed, and beds made, then everybody down to breakfast, so inspections were normally light, depending on the teacher.

A good cheat way to make your bed was to put both sheets and the blanket on, then make one hospital corner with all of them at the same time and add the cover. It would look fine during a quick inspection; the hospital corners would look a bit fat, and, if checked, you'd probably fail the inspection.

If you did fail, you could get away with just untucking the end and making the corners one at a time unless the teacher had tipped your bed or stripped it to make you do it all again in full.

Once your bed was made, you were always at risk of it being stripped for misbehaviour. Back-chatting the teacher or playing up could result in a stripping of your bed at any time.

On a Wednesday, you would be given a clean sheet, which would go at the bottom of the bed, and the sheet at the bottom would now be the top sheet.

Some of the younger boys might wet the bed; this was something you grew out of quickly at Morley Hall.

Any bedwetter would have all the boys chanting at them, and they would have to take their sheets down to the laundry and place them in a bucket of water. Your bed would then be fitted with a plastic sheet to help protect the mattress. It was deeply humiliating for any boy.

Once you completed everything, you'd line up at the top of the back stairs, ready to go down for breakfast. The floor had to all go down together, and people were hungry now, so anybody messing around was holding everybody back and delaying breakfast. You didn't want to be that boy.

With everybody ready, you could go down the stairs together and wait outside the dining room in a line for breakfast.

BREAKFAST

Once everybody was downstairs, lined up outside the dining room, you would be allowed in for breakfast. Everybody had to stand behind their chair in silence and wait for everybody to arrive, then you would be allowed to sit down, but nobody was allowed to talk until your table was served.

The tables would all be set up for breakfast; this was done the night before.

On the table, you would each have a knife to the right, a fork to the left, and a spoon at the top. On the left, there was a small plate with a butter knife on top, and above your knife, a cup and saucer.

In the middle of the table sat a large metal teapot, enough for two cups of tea each, a jug of milk, a jar of sugar, and some salt and pepper shakers.

For breakfast, you would have three courses: a

selection of breakfast cereals to choose from, then something hot, and finally some toast.

The breakfast cereals were just the basic ones you would expect at home, cornflakes, Weetabix, or Rice Krispies.

Each day the main breakfast would be something different, like scrambled eggs, beans, or spaghetti hoops; a portion would be placed on a round of toast with one other slice cut into two triangles and placed on either side.

In the winter, you might get some porridge and, if you were very lucky, gypsy toast, my absolute favourite.

The food was basic, supplied by the Norfolk County Council and nothing special, but I have never had gypsy toast made better than at Morley Hall.

If you don't know what gypsy toast is, today it's sometimes called French toast, and basically a slice of white bread dipped into an egg-milk mix and then either fried or baked.

The secret to Morley Hall's gypsy toast was the way it was cooked. In the kitchen, they had large industrial fryers used to do chips; rather than the traditional shallow frying or baking, they were deep-fried. The egg mix would splinter off and create amazing strings of fried egg.

Occasionally on a Friday, one smell would make its way around the school and cause the biggest groan—kippers. I hated kippers; we all hated kippers.

Once everybody was seated, the headmaster would then select each table, in turn, to go to the serving area and collect their cereal and return.

For the main course, the server would collect the plates from the kitchen, deliver them back to the table, and again clear them away when everybody was finished.

Finally, some more toast. Which was always cold by the time it got to the table and was delivered on a toast rack with one slice each.

You had to use your side plate for this; you would get some butter using the butter knife to put some on your plate and either some jam or marmalade using the spoon. The butter knife could only be used to put the butter on your plate, and then you could use your own knife to spread the butter.

Even at breakfast, the rules were very formal for eating to maintain discipline. Depending on the day, teachers might have some flexibility, but if the headmaster was at breakfast, everything was strictly by the rules.

One of the boys had a glass eye. At the time, his was a little smaller than it should be, and he would have a great trick to play. He would lean over your food and then open his eye wide, and his glass eye would plop into your food, perfect for getting an extra portion.

Once all the tables were cleared away, and everybody was ready, it was time to go to school.

SCHOOL TIME

From the dining room, you made your way to the locker room to put on your shoes and collect your bags, coats, and anything else you needed for school.

If you had a PE lesson that day, you would need to collect your kit. If you didn't have your own PE kit, then you would be given a Morley Hall PE kit.

The kit provided was a decade old or earlier, and nothing said 'special' like arriving to PE wearing this kit. The shorts were tied up with string rather than elastic, and the socks went up to your knees.

White socks were all the trend at the time and had been banned by the schools as they were not in the approved uniform, so the only white socks allowed were PE socks. Most pupils had modern sports brands like ADIDAS, but not Morley Hall Boys. It was really embarrassing.

In the locker room, the lockers and coat rack

were very standard, found in any school, and you got a key to keep your items safe. As with everything, they were numbered from one to thirty.

The lockers were silver-grey and a bit bashed up, something easy for the boys to punch to make a dent and a loud noise. A few were damaged from lost keys and being broken into.

Some pupils went to school lessons on-site at Morley Hall; they had two portacabin classrooms on the grounds, based in the old walled garden at the back of the site. They were used by the boys who struggled with mainstream schools for whatever reason.

The rest of the boys went to one of the traditional state schools nearby. Most went to Wymondham High, and a few went to either Attleborough or Hethersett High School.

If you went to either Wymondham or Hethersett, the minibus would take you, and if you went to Attleborough, you would walk to the end of the drive and catch the bus.

I went to one of the local state schools for my lessons and so never experienced the classrooms at Morley Hall. At school, Morley Hall Boys had a reputation for causing trouble and not being well behaved. The teachers didn't expect much from you and were just grateful if you didn't disrupt the class.

In the playground, the other kids knew you were from Morley Hall, and making friends was hard. On the plus side, you didn't get bullied; the reputation also had its advantages.

Once again, the teachers did not know what to do with me. I was frequently put in the 'special class' for pupils that were disruptive or struggling and then sent back to normal classes weeks later. The cycle just continued.

At the end of one lesson, the teacher called me back to do a little test with me and wrote down some words on a page and asked me to read them. I quickly read them out, and the teacher paused and asked me to read them again. Like magic, the words looked like they had changed, and I read them again differently. Unsure of what had happened, I looked at the teacher, very confused.

The teacher explained that something was different about the way I was seeing the words; I don't remember what he called it at the time. Over the next few months, I was frequently called out of the normal classes to meet with somebody from the Education Department who did lots of tests. I never heard of any result or anything more about it and was never given any extra help or support.

AFTER SCHOOL

Once the school day was over, it was back on the bus to Morley Hall and into the locker rooms to change your shoes.

To protect your school uniform, you were not to do anything else until you had been up to the bedrooms to get changed into your play clothes and hung up your school uniform. In the wardrobe, you would have a large wooden hanger with your number written on the top.

First, your trousers would need to be folded with the crease on the edge to keep them neat and then folded on the bottom rung of the hanger, then your shirt over the hanger with the top button done up and your tie on the top.

You would have a few hours to play on the grounds or watch some television before teatime; during this time, you had to do your homework and clean your shoes.

HOMEWORK

Wherever you went to school, you would be coming back with homework. Most of the time, you had the flexibility to do your homework whenever you wanted before teatime.

If you were a red star, you could do your homework in the red room on the ground floor between the TV room and dining room. It was smaller than the TV room and had space for around five boys. In the red room was a piano, extra games and puzzles, some nice chairs and a desk to work on, all on a very bright red carpet.

The lucky few who might be a silver star would have the silver room to work in.

Everybody else would work in the dining room; occasionally, homework was not getting done, and the schools complained to Morley Hall, and then the homework sessions would be fixed and locked down for everybody in the dining room in silence for an hour.

Once you completed your homework, it would need to be signed by a teacher to show it had been done. Some teachers' signatures were easy to fake; one teacher was so easy that he could never tell which was real and which was fake. But I never did that—well, not often.

SHOE CLEANING

Every night, you would have to clean and polish your school shoes and present them to a teacher for approval.

An old glass potting shed next to the courtyard was reserved for cleaning shoes. In the room, you would find a selection of brushes and polish in black, brown, and neutral.

For each colour, you had an 'on-brush' where you would get some shoe polish from the tin and apply it to your shoes, and then an 'off-brush' was used to buff off the polish and get a clean shine.

Once your shoes were clean, you would need to find a teacher to approve them. Cleaning shoes during playtime is not the favourite task of any twelve-year-old boy, so the quicker, the better, and the best plan was to find a soft teacher for approval. Some would glance at the shoes and be happy; others were going to take them and inspect them again and again until they were perfect. If you had been particularly badly behaved with a teacher, they might just keep finding problems for a very long time.

TEATIME

W hen the bell sounded for tea, it was time to wash your hands and line up outside the dining room again. Hands were inspected, and if the teacher couldn't smell the soap, you would be sent back to wash them again.

The routine for tea was much the same as the other meals. The menu was based on school dinners, so you had a lot of the classics with pie and mash, quiche Lorraine, baked potatoes, eggs and chips, spaghetti, and lasagne. The vegetables would be in a bowl in the centre of the table, and you were expected to have some of each; however much you might have hated cabbage, you still had to have a little.

Some of the boys would do home economics at school, sometimes called 'cooking', and bring home the food from their lessons. This was proudly reserved for your table to share, and you would be expected to present your cooking achievements. Effectively, your table would have an extra main course or dessert.

I don't know what it is about remembering school desserts, more than any other food; it can send us back in time to get our heads spinning with memories.

Chocolate sponge and custard, upside-down cake, creme caramel, jam roly-poly, treacle sponge, butterscotch, bread and butter pudding, apple crumble, sticky toffee pudding, and the classic spotted dick. One I really hated was semolina pudding; the smell and texture were awful.

Sometimes the cook made a little too much, and if it was not suitable to be kept, you might be lucky to get seconds. One of the privileges of being a higher star was getting the head of the line for seconds; the teacher would announce that we had some extras and then go down the star list until it was gone.

At the end of the meal, you would have slices of bread cut into triangles with some butter; I guess this was a way of ensuring thirty fast-growing boys were full.

I don't remember how it started, but the last slice of bread, 'the crust', was the one everybody wanted. I think it was because it was often thicker. This was normally the bottom of the pile, but the rules were clear: You could only take the next slice of bread.

The dining table was now more like a Las Vegas casino, and the slices of bread were the cards. The top prize was the last slice. With poker faces around the table, who would blink first? If you waited too long, the teacher might just end the meal and have the table cleared, so some boys just took a slice while others waited. Then with just two slices left, it was all to play for.

It was little games like these that became part of the routine of Morley Hall.

The food was on a tight budget, as you would expect from all local authority institutions; it was often at the wrong end of a joke from the boys. But we got properly fed four times a day; this was not always the case for many of the boys when they went home.

CHORES

O nce tea was finished and all the tables cleared, it was time for the headmaster or lead teacher to hand out the chores for the evening.

This was also when the teacher shared news of what was happening at Morley Hall, distributed any post, and gave updates about home weekends or planned activities. If a problem had been spotted, like any damage, everybody might get a warning.

But the main reason was to hand out the chores for the evening.

The chores were allocated in a strict number order, with no preference for your star colour, and everybody had to take their turn.

If you were on the top floor and under thirteen, you would not be asked to wash up, but you would be expected to do the drying and other tasks.

On your birthday, you would not be expected to do chores. After a while, this got expanded to allow you to have a 'free pass' from your birthday that you could use the next time your number came up. With great confidence, we convinced the teachers this was the rule, and it ran for many months, each of us using our free pass. Then one of the stricter teachers not normally assigned to teatime saw right through it all and put the rule back to birthdays only.

All the washing up needed to be done, dried, and put away, the tables needed to be cleaned, and the floor swept. The tables would need to be laid and ready for breakfast the next morning.

Jobs list, one task for each boy:

Washing crockery
Drying crockery
Washing cutlery
Drying cutlery
Cleaning dining-room floor
Laying the tables

Once dismissed from the dining room, the four boys assigned to washing up would make their way down through the kitchen into the scullery.

In the scullery, you would find the trollies filled with everything from teatime ready for cleaning. The scullery was a dark room at the end of the building facing the courtyard and had four sinks.

All the large items used to cook would have already been cleaned by the kitchen staff, and sometimes, they would have made a start on the other items for you.

The sinks were very big industrial catering units designed for large kitchens. Each boy had two sinks; one was filled with hot soapy water and the second with hot clean water.

You would wash up in the first sink and then place the items into the wire baskets designed to rack plates and cutlery. The basket was then dipped into the hot clean water to remove the soap, and the heat would make everything dry almost immediately.

Once you were done washing, the items were passed onto the dryer, who took them from the basket and polished each item by hand, removing any watermarks.

At this stage, anything not perfectly clean would be returned to the washer and done again.

Once completed, you would find a teacher to inspect everything before putting it away in the cupboards. If you had taken a few shortcuts the teacher would soon point it out.

After teatime, everybody would put their chair on the dining table to make the floor easy to sweep. Once the floor was swept, you put the chairs back, add the tablecloths and lay the tables ready for breakfast.

The teacher would inspect everything: The floor had to be free of all dirt and marks and everything perfectly laid out with each place exactly the same, ready for the morning.

FREE TIME

After tea, you had free time to play, and the grounds were very big, giving you a lot of space to roam.

The main front lawn was the old tennis court. In the summer, you could put some nets up so you could play tennis. At the back of the house was another lawn originally used for croquet.

When the weather was not as good, a games room was set up in the courtyard with table tennis, and between the locker room and the washroom was a pool table.

In the old walled garden was a concrete football pitch that flooded every time it rained. One winter, a combination of rain and hard frost turned the football pitch into an ice rink. We had great fun sliding up and down the ice. One of the boys suggested we both have a go together to see who could slide the longest. As we started the slide, he grabbed my hand and pushed it into the ice. By the time we had stopped, the skin had been ripped off my knuckles down to the bone, bleeding and very painful. I still have the scars now to remind me.

A few months later, I was looking at the fish in the concrete water tank at the back of Morley Hall. The same boy grabbed my hand and pressed it against the boiler steam vent until all the skin melted off the back of my hand. It really hurt for weeks.

In the main house was a television room with space for all the boys to sit. This was also used for meetings and the main lounge room. During the summer months, the television would be switched off, and you were told to play outside.

Like many schoolchildren around the world, on January 28, 1986, we all gathered to see the launch of the Space Shuttle Challenger as part of the Teacher in Space Project. Tragically the shuttle exploded, killing all eight astronauts, including the schoolteacher. It was quite a shock to watch this live on television.

The house was also surrounded by woodland, and one part had a large hole as if a bomb had dropped into it. The school had put a death slide and rope swing across it to play on.

Over the years, the rope failed, and one day, while I was flying around, it finally snapped and threw me into the biggest patch of stinging nettles; I was covered head to toe in little white stings and given a cold bath to help—it didn't.

One of the teachers had got a punching bag from an old boxing club and had a plan to hang it outside on the grounds on a tripod made from trees. We got permission from Wymondham College to cut down three trees from their woods, so a small group of boys got a hand saw and were tasked to cut down the trees and bring them back. The trees were huge, and it took all day to cut them down.

Once they were back, they were assembled into a tripod and lashed together with rope, and the boxing bag was then fixed in the middle; it was a great idea, and we all loved to give it a punch when angry.

Somehow, I don't think the health and safety rules today would be giving the boys a saw and sending them off into the woods.

We played a few games as teams; in the winter, a popular game was 'capture the tree', where one team would be told to protect the tree and the other team to capture it. If you touched the tree, then your team won; if the team protecting the tree touched you, then you were out. We would play this using the enormous red sequoia tree.

Sometimes the team doing the hunting would just disappear to annoy the teachers and had to be called back when nobody played the game and just one boy and a teacher were left watching the tree.

One of my favourite games was murder ball. The game was very simple: two teams and a ball. The aim was to place the ball on the opposing team's line or marker. The teacher would throw the ball in, and the game would begin. The rules were very simple: no rules.

You could do anything you liked as long as you didn't hurt anybody—well, not too much anyway. It was a great opportunity to really push your luck and do things not normally allowed. Sometimes, some of the teachers would play along.

The winner would be declared when the ball hit the marker point, and until then, anything could happen.

Once a week we might be allowed to go swimming in the Wymondham College swimming pool. This was just a short walk over the grounds, through the woods, across the boundary, and then a large building housed the indoor pool. The college kindly lent the pool once a week in the evenings, and it was great having a fully heated pool to play in.

My swimming was not great, so I spent a lot of time in the pool trying to get better. But it was not easy with around ten or twenty other boys dive-bombing, pushing others in, and trying to drown each other when the teacher was not looking.

Passed down from generation to generation of boys at the hall was the story of the secret tunnels in the woods of Wymondham College.

It was never clear what the tunnels were for, but they were out of bounds and strictly forbidden to go to. At least once a year, a few of the boys would organise a secret expedition to find them.

The site was also used for ammunition training, and spent bullet shells would make a great prized souvenir to prove you had been there.

At the end of one term, on one of the trips, a green metal ammo storage box and rifle bullet crate were found; it was full of empty shells, and I wanted it. I can't remember what it cost me; I expect I traded something for it.

I managed to fit it into a bag I was going to take home with me and then hid it away on the grounds next to the main door, so I could collect it and take it on the minibus with me home the next day.

During that day at school, I was called to the main reception and waiting for me was one of the Morley Hall staff. I was taken back and presented to the headmaster in his office.

The ammunition box was on his desk, and he wanted to know where I got it from. Somebody had grassed me up, and I knew who it was—little Jonny wanted it and could not bear that I had got it.

I was immediately demoted to a white star for the last day of term and grounded.

SHOWERS

Once playtime was over, it was time for the showers. You would collect your towel from your hook in the bathroom, and then each boy would undress, make his clothes into a bundle, and place it on the chair next to his bed.

Wrapping yourself up in your towel, you would then join the line for the shower.

Shampoo was provided twice a week on Tuesdays and Thursdays by the teacher. They would put the shampoo in your hand, one boy at a time. Under no circumstances were you allowed to get your own or touch the shampoo bottle. A bar of soap was provided, and you each had a few minutes in the shower.

The showers were communal ones; each could have two or three people at a time. It was very industrial, and the shower was either 'on or off', with little control of the pressure or temperature.

The room was tiled, and the floor painted red with big patches where the paint failed.

Getting everybody in and out of the showers and ready was never an easy task. There was no time to sort the boys by numbers or star; if you were ready, in you went. The teacher was on hand to ensure everybody had a proper wash; if you overstayed your time in the shower, you would know.

Sometimes you might want to skip the shower, so you'd have to ensure that the teacher didn't notice and that other boys did not grass on you.

A quick walk around in your towel so people saw you and a handful of water from the sink on your hair might just get you a pass.

Next, it was time to clean your teeth. Just like in the morning routine, the teacher would provide the toothpaste onto the brush and later check you had cleaned your teeth by checking if your brush was wet. If you were lazy, you might just wash your brush before putting it back in your drawer.

Headmaster David Walker, first-
floor showers (1988).

LAUNDRY

Each night, you had to change your socks and underpants, and twice a week, on Tuesdays and Thursdays, you would get a clean school shirt. At the start of each week, you would have clean school trousers and play clothes on a Friday.

Your clothes were stored away, and you would only be given the ones you would be wearing at the time.

The storeroom had a line of wooden racks, each numbered and your clothes neatly folded.

All clothing items had to have your number either written or stitched into them.

To collect your clean clothes, you had to present your dirty ones for inspection first.

Trousers were not to be inside out, and your shirt had to have all the buttons done up to the very top.

To get changed quickly, boys would undo just a couple of buttons and try to wriggle out of the shirt to reduce the work of having to do up all the buttons.

Your socks should be pinned together so they would not get separated, and the teacher would provide you with a safety pin under strict supervision.

Finally, your pants had to be inspected for skid marks.

Yes, you had to prove to the teacher you did not have any brown marks on the inside of your pants.

If you did, then you had to take your pants and wait at the top of the stairs for the skid run.

You would make your way down the backstairs and to the laundry room, which was in the courtyard between the scullery and the playroom.

Using the sink and a scrubbing brush, your job was to get your pants clean and then show them to the teacher for inspection. Once they were happy, you could leave them in a bucket of water in the laundry room.

It was normally just the younger kids on the top floor. If you were still doing this on the second floor, you would be getting your fair share of ribbing from the other boys.

At the start of one term, several boys were in the line for the skid run on the top floor, and the lead boy called everybody together for a skid train and made a big scene about it by making train noises. His plan was to be at the front, and I was at the back to ensure nobody got lost.

That night, the normal teacher was away, and we were being looked after by one of the teachers whose normal job was PE and was not somebody to mess with.

Unimpressed with the messing around, the teacher got a slipper and hit us both so hard we had a red mark on our bottoms for a week. The lead boy screamed and ran down the back staircase, back up the front staircase, and into the bedroom, still screaming.

SUPPERTIME

After everybody was showered, it was suppertime. All boys would line up outside the dining room, waiting to be called in by the teacher.

You would have a hot drink in the winter or a glass of milk if it was summer. This was a good opportunity for the school to use up leftover cakes and other food.

The drink might be hot chocolate or Horlicks and sometimes Camp Coffee.

If you have never had Camp Coffee, it is a dark brown, syrupy liquid with a smooth flavour of chicory and coffee, very sweet with a nasty chicory aftertaste. I really hated it, and it put me off coffee for life.

To eat, you would have a selection of anything that was left over, including cakes and desserts.

The supper trolley was wheeled from the

kitchen through the dining-room door.

This is where your star status really paid off. Unlike other meals where everything was the same, you had just a few of each item this time.

You were called up in star colour order, and the higher stars got the best chance of something good.

By the time you got to a blue star, you would need to get up quickly without pushing or risk getting sent to the back.

The rest just got what was left.

Occasionally the headmaster's wife, the 'matron', would try some of her experimental cooking when the kitchen staff had gone home.

One night for supper, it was a memorable fish paste she had made especially for us. 'Yummy,' we all assured her.

You can imagine the look of disappointment from the boys who were expecting an extra slice of chocolate cake.

Once finished, the plates and cups would be returned to the supper trolley for washing up.

TELEVISION

After supper, the boys would gather in the television room before bedtime.

The television room was the biggest in the house and had thirty chairs around the wall so everybody could be in the same room.

As with most of the rooms at Morley Hall, it had tall ceilings and an ornate fireplace. The windows around the room were the size of doors, each with its own wooden shutters.

The television was old and small, with no remote control, and the picture was never great. It was mounted on a large homemade trolley so everybody could see it.

We would move the chairs closer to the television to get a better view, and the teachers would tell us to move them back again.

To prevent any arguments, only a teacher could switch over the channels. We would need to find a teacher's newspaper to find a listing of what was on television, and as this was the 1980s, we only had four channels to choose from.

BEDTIME

Bedtime for the top floor was 8PM and 9PM for the second floor. Once in bed, the light switch-off would be announced, and then it was strictly no noise, no talking, and absolute silence.

A common game was to try and be the last person to talk. As the teacher announced 'good night', everybody would see who could be last to say it back. This was very annoying and could get out of hand quickly, and you could end up on the square.

The bedrooms were split over the two top floors of the house, with the younger children aged from ten to twelve on the top floor and then thirteen to sixteen on the second floor.

On the top floor, you had three bedrooms, each with five beds, a television room, shower, toilet facilities, and a clothes room.

The last bed nearest the door on the top floor was reserved for the most senior boy on that floor; they were responsible for ensuring the others knew what to do. Once you were thirteen, you moved down to the second floor.

The second floor had four bedrooms again, each with around five beds and a shower and toilet facilities. The medical room was also on the second floor, along with three bedrooms used by teachers who lived on the site.

Each bedroom had three beds on the left and then two beds on the side walls. Between each bed were a plastic chair and a small bedside table that you shared with the person next to you; you had one drawer each to store your personal items. The rooms all had a large wardrobe that you shared to hang your shirts in.

The beds were all simple single beds; I don't remember them being uncomfortable. Each was a metal frame with springs and a basic mattress and bedding. If you wanted to bring a duvet from home, that was allowed.

In the 1980s, the duvet was becoming very popular and had replaced blankets in most people's homes. However, the budget at school did not run to purchasing new bedding.

Around half of the boys had their own duvet. I had managed to perfect getting a duvet and rolling it up tightly so it would fit into the pillowcase, making it easy to transport to and from the school.

The rooms were very basic, with painted walls

that had been redecorated many times over. You spent very little time in the bedrooms; this was strictly out of bounds outside bedtimes. You were never allowed to be on a different floor to your allocated bedroom without strict permission.

If you were very lucky to be on the top floor and everybody had behaved, getting ready for bed, you might get a story. Some of the teachers liked to read a story, and for some reason, *Brer Rabbit* by Enid Blyton still sticks in my head as one of the stories told.

Headmaster David Walker in
the bedrooms (1988).

Headmaster David Walker in
the bedrooms (1988).

WEEKEND
CHORES

Weekends at Morley Hall were busy, with lots of activities to keep you from getting bored or causing trouble.

After breakfast on Saturday, we had chores to do. The teacher would read out a long list of jobs, and you would put up your hand to volunteer for that task.

If nobody volunteered, the teacher would assign somebody, and if two boys put their hands up, the boy with the higher star colour would win.

The jobs would mostly be cleaning, sweeping, polishing, or tidying spaces.

Jobs included:
Staff staircase, ground to first floor
Staff staircase, first floor to second floor

Backstairs, ground to first floor
Backstairs, first floor to second floor
Locker room
Shoe-cleaning room
Washroom
Courtyard
Door handles
Leaf sweeping
Minibus washing
Games room

And sometimes, a teacher's car might need a clean also.

Once you had been assigned your job, you would have the morning to complete it and get a teacher to inspect if the job was done correctly.

POCKET MONEY

At the weekend, you were given a little pocket money to spend. The amount went up a little depending on your age. It was less than £1 per week, and you had to collect your money from the headmaster's office, who kept a log of payments to each boy.

When the term started, and you were dropped off, your parents or guardians would give the cash to the school. Sometimes, the money would run out, and you would have to get credit from the headmaster for your pocket money.

Like many of the boys, mine ran out many times. The headmaster was often kind and let you have a little money anyway.

I expect I still owe some to Mr Walker.

TUCKSHOP

Being so remote, we didn't have much opportunity to spend our pocket money.

If you went to school outside Morley Hall, you might have the opportunity to visit a shop. Attleborough was the best school for this as you took the public bus home and got some time to visit the shops between the school and bus stop.

Morley Hall had a small tuckshop that was run by the matron. It might open for an hour over the weekend if you were lucky.

Like any little sweetshop, it contained all the favourites of penny sweets, pick'n'mix, sherbet dip dabs, and chocolate bars.

You had to form a very orderly line, and the matron would not take any trouble and would be very happy to send you away if you caused any problems.

VILLAGE SHOP

The village shop in Morley St. Peter was a twenty-minute walk from Morley Hall. Many of the roads had no paths, and the village was very small, not really big enough to support the shop, which was struggling to survive.

If you were a red star, you might get permission to walk to the shop.

It was just a village shop, but they had a much better range of sweets to buy, and the tuckshop did not always open.

Once the boys knew somebody was off to the shop, then the list of shopping would come out.

If you had some cash, then you wanted something from the shop, especially if you were below a red star or went to school in Morley Hall and never got out much.

With a pocket full of pennies and a list of items, it was off to the shop. I am not sure how the shopkeeper felt about the trip; we had to have been the most difficult customer they had with all the change and small transactions.

WYMONDHAM SHOPPING

Wymondham was the closest town to Morley Hall, and a silver star might get permission to go shopping there.

If a teacher was going to Wymondham to pick up somebody or something, you could ask for permission for a trip out with them.

With so many more shops to choose from, a trip to Wymondham would also get the list of items from the other boys.

On one shopping trip as a silver star, I was with another boy who wanted to get some birthday cards to post.

For each card he picked up and paid for, another went into his bag for free; this continued for some time, and the 'buy one get one free' offer he had invented was not a promotion the shop was running.

The theft was obvious to everybody. I was desperately trying to stop him as I was sure everybody had seen.

Not listening, he continued and then it was time to leave the shop.

As we stepped outside, the manager grabbed us and dragged us back into the shop. As I had not stolen anything, I was let go.

The teacher was also shopping, and now the race was on to find the teacher before the shop called the police.

We arrived back, and the teacher persuaded the shop manager to let him deal with the situation and assured him that the boy would be punished.

The manager agreed, and we all returned to Morley Hall. Nobody could believe it—from a silver star to a white star for shoplifting.

I never understood why he did it, and he never spoke about it. We were lucky to avoid the police that day, and I was very lucky not to be punished too.

VIDEO NIGHT

I f everybody had been really well behaved, then Saturday night might just be a movie night.

The school had a small video library of films that had been recorded from the television on the VHS video player. This was in a world before video on demand and digital recorders, and the only way to watch a movie not live on the television was to use a VHS video player. The film would be on a video cassette and put into the player connected to the television.

We had all seen the films many times; the headmaster would often record a few new ones over Christmas. If they were on the BBC, it would just be the movie, but if they had been on ITV, we might have to watch old adverts with the film if he had not paused the recording.

The collection included most of the James Bond films and the Smokey and the Bandit series.

But we wanted the new movies, and if we were very lucky, a small group would be sent with a teacher to the local video shop to rent the latest film.

Suggestions like Rambo, Die Hard, Beverly Hills Cop, Lethal Weapon, Robocop, The Terminator, or Aliens were not welcomed by the teacher as we had to have a film that was suitable for the top floor and boys under thirteen.

In the shop, we each selected a film we liked and then it was a negotiation about which one we would take home. First, we had to persuade the other boys that our film was the best choice and then the teacher that it would be acceptable for everybody.

The teacher often took the rating on the video as guidance, and if they were happy, we could choose a film with a higher rating.

I really hoped it was not another Kung Fu movie as the older boys would be trying to chop you for days later.

Once the film was chosen, it was back to Morley Hall to tell everybody. You never found a film everybody was happy with; some had seen it, and some didn't want to see it, and if it was a flop, you knew about it.

When everybody was ready for bed, the tape was played from the VHS machine in the headmaster's office, and the cable went to the ground-floor television room and then up to the third-floor television room for the younger boys.

We had our fair share of duds and flops, but I also remember some classic movies from the 80s.

CHURCH

Sunday was church day, and all the boys were expected to walk to church.

We had three churches that would normally hold a service on Sunday.

The closest, Morley St. Peter, was a fifteen-minute walk, Morley St Botolph's was a twenty-five-minute walk, and the Morley Methodist Church was a fifteen-minute walk.

Both St Botolph's and St. Peter were Church of England and traditional old English village churches, and the Methodist Church was a more modern build.

For church, we had to wear our school uniform, so we did not mess it up; the boys would change just before the walk to the church and then again as soon as we got back.

The roads were very narrow, just wide enough for a tractor, and cars frequently hit birds and animals. When walking to the church, one of the boys found a pheasant that had been clipped by a car. It was still alive but in distress. He picked up, wrung its neck, and threw it into the field, all very casually, as if he'd found a tree branch in the road and wanted to move it.

Nobody really liked going to church. Even if you came from a religious family, the church was very old, and the vicar had little in common with our lives. The service had not changed much for decades, and it was eating into your weekend.

You were on your best behaviour in church; the teachers did not accept any messing around and would be very unhappy to be embarrassed in front of the vicar or the local congregation.

By the 1980s, the local village churches were not used much for services and numbers were falling. The service might have a dozen people at the most, so arriving with thirty boys really boosted the numbers.

I don't know if the vicar was pleased that we came to the church or if they knew we were coming. To us, it was all very boring, the sermons were long and dull, and the hymns made no sense to us at all.

One of the vicars did make an effort with more friendly, happy hymns and some of the more popular stories from the Bible.

If we went to the Methodist Church, they were more modern and ran a Sunday school, but we never went very often.

During the service, they would pass around the collection plate, and you were expected to put something in. Even if it was just a penny or two pence, everybody had to drop a coin in the collection. If you did not have a coin, you would have to borrow from another boy or teacher.

One Sunday, the vicar gave a talk about not wasting food and reminded us to eat all our crusts. This caused a ripple of laughter from the boys, and the vicar stopped to try and understand why.

The teacher had to explain how we fought for the crusts at the end of a meal.

The vicar looked after many churches, and very occasionally, his service was in a church too far away for us to walk. One weekend when this happened, the teachers didn't tell us the service was cancelled and made us walk to Morley St. Peter to find the church closed, then to Morley St. Botolph's to another closed church, and then back to Morley Hall. We were all quite tired from the walking and the teachers rather pleased with themselves and their deception.

In September would be the harvest festival service, and the front of the church would be filled with the incredible range of crops grown in Norfolk in celebration of the harvest.

The church would donate some of the food to Morley Hall, and for some reason, every year, it was the pumpkin. Great, if you wanted to carve out a nice face, add a candle, and put it on the drive. But not Morley Hall; we had to eat it, and I hated pumpkin. Do you know just how many recipes you can make? Pumpkin pie, pumpkin cake, pumpkin soup, stuffed pumpkin, roast pumpkin, pumpkin stew, and pumpkin pasta.

It felt like the pumpkin lasted forever and would never end. Just how big was this pumpkin?

SUNDAY DINNER

Sunday was roast dinner day. The best meal of the week and something Morley Hall did really well.

The best roast dinners are made with a large cut of meat slow-roasted in the oven together with roasted potatoes, mash, seasonal vegetables, and homemade Yorkshire puddings with lashings of gravy.

Then a classic steamed pudding with custard followed for dessert.

For all the jokes the boys made about Morley Hall food, the Sunday roast was always something special; somehow, I don't think we really appreciated how good it was.

After Sunday dinner came the washing-up chores, and then we had the afternoon to play in the grounds.

TRIPS OUT

At the weekend, we might get taken out in the minibus for a trip somewhere.

Normally it was a large open space where we could all run around and tire ourselves out.

Norfolk has plenty of great spaces like Mousehold Heath in Norwich or Castle Hill in Thetford; Cromer beach was not too far, and Thursford had a great play area for visitors.

The trip would be announced at dinner, and you would put your hand up if you wanted to go.

You could fit around fifteen in the minibus, and normally, only boys who were a blue star and above would be allowed to go on trips.

The minibus was always so slow, and each journey felt like it took forever to get anywhere. The boys could get restless on the journey, and it wasn't easy to manage for the teachers. I am surprised they took us out at all, given the trouble we could cause.

Once you arrived, the teacher set the rules for the visit: how long we could stay, what time to be back at the bus, where you could go, and what was out of bounds.

CHRISTMAS

Everybody at Morley Hall made a big effort to make Christmas as nice as possible. As it was also the end of term, everybody would be very excited to go home and celebrate.

The building had huge ceilings, perfect for putting up a massive Christmas tree. The tree would be covered with all the traditional decorations and lights and look amazing in the main hallway, especially at night with all the colourful lights.

Around the rest of the building, we would have the opportunity to dress the rooms and even make some of the decorations.

In the run-up to the end of term, we had a school disco. This was the only time we had a 'party' of any sort; the teachers spent most of the year trying to ensure we did nothing of the sort.

The main television room would be emptied;

this shared a removable wall with the red room to make it into a much bigger space. The disco kit would be set up in the red room with the music kit and all the lights, and the dance floor would be the television room.

As this was a boys-only school, we needed to invite some girls to the party.

Fortunately for us, the Norfolk Education Department had another school for girls, Colne Cottage in Cromer.

Colne Cottage was the same as Morley Hall; they had taken thirty girls, all with the same problems and put them all together.

The girls would arrive from Cromer in their minibus for the disco. It was all a bit awkward as nobody knew each other, and we all stuck to our side of the room, trying to size each other up.

Eventually, with a little persuasion from the teachers, some of the boys would be chatting to the girls and dancing.

A few would try and disappear for a little more than dancing, and the teachers from both sides would keep an eye out and check where everybody was.

It always felt like the disco ended just as we had all got to know each other, and the party was just getting started.

Bundled back on the bus, the girls were sent back to Cromer, and the boys were left to clean up everything and share a few stories from the encounter.

Christmas is not Christmas without a massive celebration dinner, and Morley Hall was no exception. The last weekend before the end of term would be our Christmas dinner.

The dining room would be decorated, and the tables laid out with crackers and hats. If you are going to have the best Christmas dinner, then you need to go to Norfolk. It's where the turkeys are from, the potatoes grow, and the best seasonal vegetables are harvested.

Every table space was taken by the boys and teachers, and the room was filled with an atmosphere of celebration with turkey, pigs in blankets, roasted potatoes, mash, Yorkshires, cranberry sauce, and Christmas pudding.

Our Christmas celebrations would end with two school plays from the boys who had their classes at Morley Hall.

This was always a big night, and the two classes would have put in a lot of effort to rehearse.

While many of the boys might have issues with school and not be the best with their reading and writing, some were very creative.

The television room was converted into a theatre with all the chairs facing the red room, which was used as the stage, and the dividing doors as the curtain.

I still remember a few of them today.

In one play, the class had put up a giant white sheet to cover the room entrance and bright lights to make everything in silhouette.

Their story unfolded with a series of characters and props they had made that all worked perfectly with the shadows.

In another, the Norfolk Education Department food was the target of some fun, and the song 'Morley Hall cheese comes bouncing back to me…' still rings in my head today.

Not wanting to be left out, one year, I decided to put on my own play. Why should all the fun be reserved for the classes based at Morley Hall?

A small group of us who went to one of the external schools all agreed to write and perform our own little sketch show. One of the boys played the piano, and we were all happy to sing a bit and tell a few jokes.

Add in a little bit of falling over and some custard pies, and we were ready.

We practiced lots and knew all of our steps; we even did the play in silence to test how well we knew where to stand and when.

On the night, everybody was on their best behaviour as the head of the Norfolk Education Department had been invited and surprisingly actually came.

The plays were going well, and I was in the kitchen with some eggs, making the meringue to throw.

Then word came from one of the teachers that our play would not be allowed to go on. They said it was overrunning and short of time. But the matron had got word about our play and did not trust us one bit—especially with the guest from the Education Department—and so we never got to perform it.

After the last day at school before the Christmas break, we made our way back to Morley Hall, ready to go home for Christmas.

All the decorations had already been taken down, and the tree was gone as if Christmas was already over.

LEAVING
MORLEY HALL

In July 1988, age fifteen, I did my exams and left Morley Hall for the last time.

This was the first year of the new-style GCSE exams, and I had studied for eight of them; the results would be out in August.

Whatever the results, this was the end of education for me; I wanted nothing else to do with schools, sixth form, colleges, or universities.

I hated my time at school; it was not the best part of my life for so many reasons. Once released from Morley Hall, I ran as far away as I could. I wanted the freedom to do what I wanted when I wanted and to get away from the authorities and authority. I have kept running ever since and never stopped.

For as much as I hated my school years, we were

all very lucky to be at Morley Hall. I was very lucky to be at Morley Hall.

Whether escaping from problems at home or school, all of us boys had been given a chance to get a better start in life as adults.

Morley Hall was a last-chance warning; a Borstal, young offenders, or prison would be the next step if we did not learn to follow the rules.

Before leaving Morley Hall, the headmaster had a tradition of taking the boys who were leaving that year out for dinner at the local Indian restaurant in Attleborough. I had never been to a restaurant for dinner before, so this was an amazing experience for me. We got to look at this magical menu of food from India and try things we had never eaten before.

On my final day at Morley Hall, I checked my locker and personal box, packed all my things away, and was ready to leave.

I would be the last to get off the minibus that day—the end of the road. Driving the bus was Peter, one of the nicer teachers, who was very sensible and cared about the boys.

He shook my hand, and I was surprised as it was not something I had experienced before. He wished me good luck, and with that, I was free to leave.

My time at Morley Hall was over.

THE END

FURTHER READING

***A Shilling, A Shutknife And A Piece Of String* by Wigby Frederick C.**
Frederick Wigby details his life, including working at Morley Hall in the 1950s.

***Morley Hall Boy* by John Dyble**
John Dyble looks at his time as a boy at Morley Hall in the 1960s.

ACKNOWLEDGEMENTS

I would like to thank everybody who has helped make this book possible, including Julie Bass, Robert Green, Jon Heggie, Ana Joldes, Ana Hantt, Josie Baron, Rebecacovers, Mike Christensen, James Hourd, Amel Kelkouli, Dave Morgan, Jess Bogdan, Maryam, Yoanna, Darren Deans, Emma Cartledge from Norfolk County Council, Norfolk Record Office, Jamie Lambert from GSD Lambert & Sons Limited, and all the staff and boys of Morley Hall.

Printed in Great Britain
by Amazon